Once my sister lost a shoe of hers at the playground while playing on the swings. My family and I would pass our school and we'd always say "I wonder what happened to Vera's shoe." It was a memorable moment and we laughed about it every time.

I swear we could not find it.

Finding Faith and Hope

Finding Faith and Hope

a

Memoir

Nadya Carlson-Bowen

FOR V

STRENGTH AND BEAUTY ALWAYS

Published by: Nadya Carlson-Bowen with assistance from
Peter A Blacksberg

This is a personal recollection and all text is mine, unless otherwise credited.

ISBN: 9781674835051

Cover photograph by Nadya Carlson-Bowen

For copies and more information contact:
Nadya Carlson-Bowen at FindHopeandFaith@gmail.com

First Edition

First printing on December 18, 2019

PREFACE

We are in a sunflower field as these are our favorite flowers. There she was across at a distance. I run to her screaming "Sissy!", and she smiles and waves to me. She says, "I have to go, but I love you." Then she disappears into the fields.

I remember waking up crying in tears because at that exact moment I felt her presence with me. Visits are real and if you believe in them, they will happen. I never thought of this as a coincidence. This visit was showing me my sister wanted to let me know she was okay. I still visit sunflowers fields because of her. They are so magical and just beautiful to watch in a big field. They are strong, stand tall and are so beautiful. That reminds me of what my sister was – strong and beautiful.

They say the first five years of your life are important. It shapes you to start being who you will become when you are older. I agree and will start there.

CHAPTER 1

1989 – ST PETERSBURG, RUSSIA: WE ARE BORN

It was a cold place and I had no family. The buildings are so beautiful. St. Petersburg is a combination of Venice, Miami and Paris. Paris, because of its architecture, Venice because of the canals, and Miami because the buildings are painted in pastel colors. It is a very beautiful bright place, but COLD! A lot of snow everywhere.

Starting Life in Russia

Imagine yourself three years old with rooms having golden beds to sleep in, your slippers under your bed, and the walls painted with old fashioned patterns. Thinking back to my earliest years, these were the small beds we slept in, a small playroom to play in and a very tiny bath-

Our bedroom

room shared by so many. Playing with a lot of children and seeing our caregivers engage with us was rough as the ratio was nothing like a real family with about five grown-ups to 25 children. There are orphanages throughout Russia. The caregivers taught us to have very good manners and to recite poetry. We could memorize and sing long songs. We were on a daily schedule meaning that every child did everything together (brushing teeth, getting ready for bed, getting ready for the day, and eating meals). The caregivers provided the best they could for all of us, and sometimes it was just not enough.

This was the orphanage I came from St. Petersburg, taken in at five months old. My birth parents were very sick, and so they thought it was best for me to be placed there. My birth father passed shortly after I turned one year old and they looked for my birth mother for the first few years of my life but had no luck in finding her. Luckily, I had one special person to share this life with me.

We sensed we had a permanent bond from the start. We laughed, played and learned to grow up loving each other. Living in the orphanage we had each other which of course helped us both. We were our closest friends. Then. . . Surprise! I learned she was my twin. We were fraternal of course but looked a lot alike. Back then we were too young to understand we were sisters, much less twins. We were best friends. Her name was Vera.

Though we were very young, I remember there were some good memories we shared. I got to take care of a yellow parakeet as that was part of my "job" at the orphanage. Vera and many others would rotate in cleaning dollhouses for us to understand how to clean and manage household responsibilities.

There are other memories. In Russia, they believed every child should feel powerful and strong through rough times. This was the beginning that prepared us for the challenges we would face. The founder of St. Petersburg did this and believed dunking children's heads in cold water made us healthier. So, they dunked us in freezing cold water to show we could get through it. This did not go well, but that's another story to tell sometime later. No other tough love ever happened. In those early years, there were caregivers taking care of us while growing up in the orphanage. Then something happened.

Our new Mom and Dad

CHAPTER 2

1995 – OUR LIVES RESTART: ADOPTION

At age five, Vera and I were adopted from St. Petersburg by two loving parents, Peg and Paul, from California. I could laugh and cry at the same time. I mean, what an adventure! It was a whole new experience for us both, as well for our new parents.

Our adoptive parents had their own laughs and cries along the way to adopting two Russian girls. Though at times they didn't know if they would succeed in adopting us. There could be a big chance that our new parents would come to Russia, also knowing they couldn't adopt us. That's the chance our new parents took when flying over to meet us. Peg and Paul said they wanted two girls. Our adoptive mom mentioned to the agency that she wanted girls with personalities and the adoption agency responded to my adoptive parents, the two girls they thought were a good match, that they were not shy at all. The Russian Federation was making sure that we were adopted together. They were very serious about keeping us twins together.

Paperwork and more paperwork!

My new mother had heard about my sister and me at an adoption conference and she called them, and they sent her our pictures. She knew these twins were meant for them. Throughout the adoption process, my parents went back and forth with counseling, therapy, signing papers, seeing photos of us and getting ready for a long, long trip. The adoption process followed - from domestic adoption to international, foster care, pre-adoption meetings to home studies required for my adoptive parents. The paperwork was a total nightmare.

For us, it meant all new words and language to learn and understand. There were so many steps into this beautiful process! I remember back then in the orphanage they would show us photos of our adoptive parents and tell us that they were our parents.

The moment they got to the orphanage, we saw them in the distance. We both went running into their arms saying "Mama! Papa!" changing our lives forever. We were hooked, and it was such an impactful moment.

Our next words and only our words in English were "Good morningk." The little "k" on the end of "morning" remained for some time and only served to make us more endearing. The caregivers met my adoptive parents and were so happy for us. There were about 25 children in that orphanage and hundreds in other locations.

While wrapping up their first visit, my adoptive parents played with us in a large room with a large rubber ball and we constantly rolled up and down on it while falling off of it laughing hysterically.

After, we shared cookies and tea with the caregivers and also the director of the orphanage too. This led to very bad teeth for Vera and me. Because we had very poor nutrition, Vera had no teeth and when we went to our first dentist appointment in our new country, I had 14 cavities.

We arrive in California

CHAPTER 3

ENTERING THE SOCIAL WORLD OF OUR NEW PARENTS

Leaving Mother Russia . . .

After leaving St. Petersburg, Moscow, on the train, we then took the plane from Moscow to New York. The orphanage paid for a Russian soldier to protect us on the train.

In New York City we saw our first African American, and as five-year-old Russian girls we thought they were made out of chocolate, just because we had never seen any African Americans before. This was just all so new to us– a person with a different skin color.

In the Moscow airport, my adoptive parents knew our passport pictures were swapped and worried that this would prevent us from getting on the plane. The security agents checked our passports eleven times and they still didn't notice the swap, but that's how much alike we looked then. While waiting at the airport, this gentleman who was in line at security with us, who was also Russian, mentioned to our parents that my twin and I spoke Russian very well and my mom laughed and replied, "That's because they are Russian."

The flight from Russia to the United States was long, especially for our new parents but also long for us. We had never been on an airplane before. We cried all the way on the flight. It was all new to us and we had not known what flying was!

We finally arrived at the Atlanta airport. In the terminal, we were screaming and running around and eventually, my mom picked us both in each of her arms trying to carry us from one concourse to the other to get us settled in to wait for the flight to California. My mom still has flashbacks to this day and says it was not fun at all.

After that experience, we finally got on the plane and as a family we sat right behind identical twin ministers. They were a singing act and traveling around the country. My parents said to them, "Move now, our kids are going to be noisy the whole flight, so we won't be offended if you move." They responded with, "We don't mind, it'll be fine." After the ministers said that, we didn't make a single sound the whole flight. At the end of the flight, my mom asked them "You prayed, didn't you?" Both ministers responded, "Yeah, you should have done that in Moscow too."

Flying over all is a hassle but it can also be very easy. Now you can envision how hard it must have been for the family to experience flying together for the first time - a little bit of both. So it was, on January 24th 1995, we arrived in our new home, a world away from everything we had known.

Hope and Faith ornaments

CHAPTER 4

ADAPTING FROM THE RUSSIAN CULTURE

In San Jose, California, our house looked completely different from what we ever lived in before. It had a vintage look; a dark brown wooden garage door and a cream color painted outside. I remember on our garage door, there was a "Welcome Home" sign for Vera and me. There was much warmer weather year round no snow of course. It felt like home for us because it was so welcoming and comforting. We had no issue in settling in the house and adjusting. I remembered we would explore every room a feeling full of excitement! As we entered our new home, on the right was our living room, and a tall green Christmas tree standing there. Even though it was late January, our Christmas tree was still up the day we arrived home. Our bedroom walls were painted blue, our beds had white bedposts and frames and the bedding was poofy and fluffy.

Our bedroom felt very cozy. It was weird sharing a bedroom with only one other person. I recall shortly after arriving and seeing our bedrooms we started to cry hysterically. My mother looked at us and said, "What did I do now?" We looked at her and responded, "We don't have slippers under our bed." and cried. That was something that meant so much to us, and yet unknown to our parents. Many small things that we took for granted in the orphanage were missing or different in our new home.

In the orphanage children would go to bed, but we never saw an adult go to sleep, so when we first saw our parents go to sleep in our new home we started crying again because we simply didn't know about adults having to sleep. In our minds, we thought for adults, sleeping meant dying so we didn't understand the actual meaning behind sleep.

Not long ago after we were adopted and settled into our new home, we met a lot of family at our grandmother's house and it was a wonderful experience for all. I remember us wearing colorful dresses, dancing and playing with our new family. We were talking in Russian as if our whole family knew the language, but they didn't. Meeting our new family was so exciting for us and probably so exhausting for everyone else with the energy we had. My sister was the energetic, social one. She met people on the spot and chatted away in Russian, whereas I was a bit more shy. I warmed up to people in time.

I remember we had two kitties who lived with us – Rita and Tyler. They were Siamese kittens. Rita used to hate us because we'd chase her around the house, and we'd find Tyler in the laundry basket all the time. Rita was very timid, probably because we chased her everywhere, and Tyler grew up to be a cat with a heartwarming personality and loved everyone. I think the reason we enjoyed having pets in our home was because I experienced it in the orphanage. However, when I was little, I was terrified of dogs, and we still don't know why, but I was. They do have big Russian security dogs in Russia that protect people there so maybe that's why. Fortunately, I grew past that fear and we've had many friendly pet dogs since.

Learning all sorts of different things including language was the biggest transition for us both. However, translating English to Russian, I learned at a much slower pace than my twin. Vera then would translate everything into English for my parents. After watching endless Disney movies we had dinner conversations filled with lines we memorized. My parents were laughing. Disney was a big part of our lives once we got to our new home. Watching Disney movies was on the agenda for most days. Here's a funny memory; As with all moms sometimes my mom would make me mad. One time when I thought she was being really mean, but I didn't know how to say it in English, I just looked at my mom and pointed at her and said "Cruella De Vil". We all know where that's from!

Dressed as Esmérelda & Minnie mouse

We also enjoyed watching Barney, and for some reason, it was very hard for us to say Barney. We somehow couldn't say the 'e' final sound. There are not many Russian words that ended in "e" but a lot of words that end with 'ic'. So we pronounced Barney, "Barnic."

Playing dress up

Playing at our local park in San Jose, California

CHAPTER 5

SCHOOL

In kindergarten, we did what every twin would imagine ever doing to our teachers. Our parents always dressed us in the same clothing, so we would occasionally switch classes to throw off teachers. I learned a lot in kindergarten. I learned how to socialize in a new world with new people. Once my sister lost a shoe of hers at the playground while playing on the swings. My family and I would pass our school and we'd always say, "I wonder what happened to Vera's shoe." It was a memorable moment and we laughed about it every time. I swear we could not find it. We repeated Kindergarten another year because our teachers thought it was best to make sure our English was better before moving to first grade.

Schooling was definitely a new experience for us but we managed to like it, most of the time. English was, of course, our second language so it did take some time to understand the new language. We had very supportive teachers in all the schools we attended and learned at different paces from each other. In fact, I had a different learning disability than my sister but we managed our learning disabilities with different solutions the schools provided for us. For example, when I would try and explain something to someone, I would get frustrated at being unable to explain my English correctly to others, because processing it down from my brain to paper would be difficult for me to do. Later I was trying to write and found out I have a form of Dyslexia. Today I still struggle with this disability but it's definitely improved over the years.

When Vera and I were in second grade our teachers used to have to ask Vera to give me a chance to talk, since she wanted to talk all the time. She was very quick with her words and I seemed to take my time formulating and expressing what I wanted to say. I was pretty patient with my sister at this age, even though she was always speaking for me. My sister had a strong personality and was always looking out for me. Eventually, I learned to hold my

own and by 4th grade we were both strong, funny, loving individuals. Vera struggled with academics, however, she always had a smile on her face. Her struggle with schooling never brought her down. Twins can look alike, but they are their two different kinds of people. That's what we were.

Vera only liked school for the social part, and I was there to learn. Vera was truly a daredevil. At recess, the boys used to be intimated by her acrobatic flips off the playground monkey bars. Scary moves that had the principal calling our mom. Then again perhaps I wasn't an angel all the time. I remember having a substitute teacher one day and I remember a few of my friends and I went off campus thinking that the substitute teacher wouldn't know, but we got caught. Yes, I did that, not the trouble maker Vera.

Also, rarely ever our teachers put us in the same classroom and most teachers who know siblings tend to learn better separately. When we were together I had to be "like" Vera and when I was separated I could be myself. Everything also was a competition to us in school. For example, we'd fight over the best answer or who was smarter. Some of the class thought it was funny, others found it annoying. We learned differently too. When we were separated, we also had a different outlook on school while being educated which caused us to learn differently. From my experience, my thoughts having a sibling in your class only leads you to one thing, socializing. When siblings are placed in separate classes it allows each to focus on him or herself. They improve academically being independent, rather than always doing what the other one wants.

As we learned to get adjusted to our new home, over time, my parents knew we had to be in sports and they figured out how to get us involved.

We were always so full of high energy. Our first sports experience was exciting! In the orphanage, we were taught great social skills that developed our social skills for sports so being welcomed on teams or being social, was not a problem for us. It was also nice to be born naturally athletic. We first tried T-ball, Dance, gymnastics, and soccer. We loved all the sports we tried, but managing a schedule with two girls and four sports was very tough on us and our parents. So we stayed with one sport. Then it came down to a sport where one of our soccer coaches said: "These girls need a sport where they can run." We would manage to finish up the sport and whatever sport or activity it was, we still had so much energy left. So then it was determined that soccer was a natural sport for us.

What began playing soccer in grade school and continued all the way through college. We shared so many wonderful memories. Playing with each other, we discovered twins really did have superpowers. It was known as the soccer twin connection. We were unstoppable! So fun to play together. We played on two teams growing up: taking one team seriously and learning to grow and develop our skills while our second team was all fun and games where this team felt like family.

We played on teams such as Lightning, Surf-Girls, Torpedos, Wild Cats and many others. The primary team we played on for many years and grew up with was the Surf-Girls. (This was because both Vera and I were one year older than the other younger players that it made us age out every other season, so we'd play with this team every other season.) While playing for fun, we played on a competitive team to keep our skills up. We were playing a lot of soccer! Both teams we played for were the highlights of our youngest years. Soccer is what helped us keep going and doing well in life. I believed it was the best decision for us to be put in this sport because it helped us so much with everything. It allowed us to get involved and interact with our peers and friends which at the age of five where we just came from Russia, this was a good social activity for us to make new friends. This can help any child adjust to life in a better way. I still remember when we were added to the team, we just wanted to play, but our coaches knew we had a passion for this sport and it would take us far!

Childhood in California held lots of new experiences for us! Thinking back it was Christmas time when we arrived in the United States which is why I love Christmas to this day. Actually, we arrived home on January 24th. and it felt Christmas to us because our tree was still up. This was our first Christmas together as a family. With the songs being overplayed, California fake snow being displayed, hot cocoa or peppermint to drink, and much joy in the air. It is such a happy time in our lives celebrating together with new friends and family.

It was also the time when I recalled the Russian language as I remembered Russian Christmas songs. Later I remember talking with my twin and figuring out how Santa comes to all the houses on Christmas day and delivers presents. Vera shouted out with excitement and in a judgemental tone, "Mom and Dad can't afford all these presents, it has to be Santa that brings them all, our parents are too cheap." We all started to crack up. Crying so hard our cheeks turned red and our eyes filled up. It was never the same again!

For many who are adopted, the day they are adopted is called "Gotchya Day" (Got you day). Ours came right after Chirstmas. Each year, on Gotchya Day we did something fun as a family. In-time made a tradition of going out for dinner at Max's restaurant. We loved it!

After almost learning English and leaving Russian language behind, I remember another time the language came back to me – the first time we went ice skating. Hot cocoa, ice, and friends all having fun. I passed my mother and said "Paca mama". Which means goodbye in Russian. The ice and cold brought back memories while living in Russia.

Clearly a lot had happened and there was a lot to adjust to our new world. There was our first visit to a zoo. I had never experienced animals at a zoo. This was hilarious!

My first zoo outing went like this – We got to the zoo and I was very disappointed because I thought the zoo provided animals to care for or to even take home. Well, that changed very quickly! I'd get up to a cage and say "Mama, it's a tiger!" Mama would respond, "Yes it is." I would then ask, "Can I touch it?" Mama responded, "No." "Can I feed it?" Again Mama said, "No." "Can I take it home?" Mama responded, "No." I threw up my hands in the air and huffed and said, "Well what's the point?"

Many years later giraffes are still our favorite animal. Mom and me looking on as Dad gives a treat at the San Francisco Zoo.

20

Unfortunately, it didn't stop, I went to every cage and did that. This was my perspective when it came to visiting a zoo for the first time.

I even remember experiencing our first trip to Disneyland. We went to Disney to meet characters and I remember Vera always being picked by Disney performers for the Disneyland events where I would quietly raise my hand. For me, it wasn't the end of the world not to be picked. She would get picked for everything and my parents would pray to have them pick me and feel bad it was always Vera.

It was 1999, we were 10 years old. That year the Women's Professional National Soccer Team won the World Cup. We were so excited! Mom and dad drove us to the San Jose airport, and we waived to Brandi Chastain and the Women's National Team. This was the first time we met our idol and legendary soccer player Brandi Chastain. Later, my dad ended up working with the Women's Professional Soccer League (WPSL). Brandi Chastain has been a good long-time friend to our family and she was one big idol to Vera and me while we grew up playing soccer. We went to all of her soccer camps when we were young! She was the reason we played and had such a beautiful passion for the sport.

Dressed as monkeys for Jungle Book dance recital.

CHAPTER 6

PRE-TEEN YEARS

As we got older, the Russian language faded away and we were speaking English most of the time. It's part of a bonding process for foreign adoptees to reject their culture and fit in. It was expected and actually a healthy thing at that stage. I remember my mom asking us to go to Russian culture events and we both refused to go!

Many of our schools had extra activities/curricula for the students. Vera and I took dance. The CPAC (Center of Performing Arts) had many dance recitals offered through our school. We starred in Beauty and the Beast, The Jungle Book, Peter Pan and more.

As we entered our pre-teen years, we still played soccer and continued through our school years. Then in 6th grade, we graduated to middle school. Adjusting to middle school was a big change for us as it is for everyone. All our lives we had our elementary school friends with us. You know, in middle school many children do not go to the same school as you, so the social groups can change from very little or a lot. We had bigger classes and a harder schedule to manage, but we succeeded just fine.

We had different social groups and found we were still being confused for one another by friends and teachers. They seemed to not be able to tell us apart. I thought this was strange because Vera was the type of student known for being the class clown, and I was more into being quiet. Even though we had our personal differences and different friends, we always had each other. It's good to have a friend and in this case a sibling with you in a new transition. It makes it easier on yourself and helps you feel more encouraged in being able to complete the school year with someone you know.

I never thought I would have played another sport other than soccer, but I tried out for volleyball my middle school years and I made the team. Vera wanted to play basketball so she did that. I still remember the half-court shot she made at the final buzzer and it was such an amazing fun moment to share with her team! We were natural at sports and always just wanted to have fun with them. Even competing against boys at this age was fun, because they would always underestimate us!

Celebrating birthdays for us was the best too. We had probably every birthday at the Aloha Roller Rink every year. Even when we tried to change it for a new birthday experience, last minute it would be at Aloha. It was typically more of Vera's environment as she was just so natural at every sport. I was not a roller skater, but it was what Vera wanted and I just went with it. Each year was like a reunion with many friends who surrounded us on our birthdays!

Hugs after our soccer game

CHAPTER 7

TEENAGERS

In our teenage years was when our interests grew apart but that was okay. Even if you're twins, you still can be interested in different things. I remember I was a bookworm and my first two years of high school, I did well in school.

Vera was more of the social gal, and she thought that was the way to be successful in high school. We had set different goals for ourselves. Even so, we continued playing soccer in these years. Through high school we played both for the school team and Club soccer. Club soccer was extramural and many of our close friends played on the same soccer team while growing up. Club soccer was not as competitive as our school team was. We continued to play Club soccer and two years of high school soccer.

As much as we loved playing soccer, we waited until our junior year. When we played for our high school, our coach asked us "Why didn't you both come out for your first two years of high school and play?". We hesitated and both stated, "We didn't like the previous coach." Our coach, Randy took over as the head coach right before we joined, so he didn't know about the old coach. Randy looked at us and rolled his eyes because he saw potential in us both. I ended up playing defense for the majority of the time then managed to use my speed and skills to play offense, except then I would be needed to play defense. The coach would put me in offense, and I'd go back and play defense. I was being moved around in all positions for soccer. I grew up understanding the different positions such as offense (attacking with the ball) and defense (defending against players).

Vera was the showoff queen with the fancy moves where I was more tactical and played off with speed. Vera would always try and beat players with *around-the-world* where a player tries to beat the defender with a move. I knew her moves. So when I would defend her during practice it made it that much easier. She was also less of a team player, relying more on her own one-girl moves, rather than passing the ball and sharing the glory. The coach would bench her for it until she learned how to work as part of a team. I found myself more willing to share the ball on the field. I supposed we balanced each other in this way. We were this way on and off the soccer field.

In my senior year I had a bad injury, landing wrong on my right ankle. I ended up coming out of the game for about five minutes and eager to go back in and play. I played every minute of the second half. It wasn't till the next day I woke up with a swollen and bruised broken ankle. Yup, broken. Pain sometimes doesn't affect you then, but it'll affect you later. When athletes play sports they have an athlete mind of their own where they want to play through injuries. This was definitely one of those moments. This also made me miss the Senior Showcase*. And of course, guess who the coach picked. . Vera.

I was happy that Vera was chosen but disappointed I couldn't play.

*Senior Showcase select two top seniors from each school to play in a game with about two dozen other players in our district. Soccer scouts from two year or four-year colleges came to watch students play.

CHAPTER 8

BECOMING ADULTS

We turned 21 years old and shared a great birthday together. We celebrated the night before our birthday and Vera didn't even make it to midnight to celebrate. We all laughed. This was our first time drinking publically at age 21. Maybe a bit too much?

As I turned the corner into adulthood, I started to think about what I wanted to do in the future. Up until then, it had been soccer, coaching and nannying. I worked with many families being a nanny and also coached soccer. I remembered it took me a few job interviews to find the perfect family to nanny for. I had one family where the children were crazy, and I had to tell them I needed to quit. It was my only first week with them. At that time my sister played soccer and worked at a restaurant. We also got our driver's license at this time. Some young adults are too lazy to get their licenses, that wasn't us. Both my sister and I just couldn't pass the test. We both had learning disabilities growing up and we don't do well on tests. I finally passed the exam, getting mine first and drove my sister around till she got hers. I remember I had to drive her everywhere before she got hers a few weeks later. . .Finally!

We are captured playing Evergreen College on the West Valley Vikings.
That's me on the right.

CHAPTER 9

2009 – WE ENTER COLLEGE & THROUGH OUR COLLEGE YEARS

After high school, both Vera and I were scouted to play at West Valley. Being a student athlete meant a lot. You had to keep up with grades in order to play sports. This wasn't too big of a struggle for me, but again Vera just wanted to play soccer and socialize. School still wasn't her thing.

We took classes together and again it wasn't the best. I felt I could take control at this age and focus more with V in my class, however, Vera made class more fun trying to always distract everyone else from learning. After a couple of years of school at West Valley, I got a scholarship to play soccer in a four-year program. I went to several player ID camps that other coaches watch you play. Vera was very supportive of me. I remember her coming to my games. She decided at this point to take school off and work at a restaurant. This is when she knew she'd start working in this business. Sadly I had a tough hamstring injury just right after I signed with the Holy Names University Hawks. I ended up redshirting for the semester and returning to West Valley to finish up my schooling. The school just wasn't a fit for me. While I was doing this, Vera had decided to get back on her feet and start college again as motivation from myself and family. It wasn't a couple of semesters later we found out she had Cancer.

Posing for the US National Soccer Team

Celebrating Dad's 70th birthday together. Our last as a family.

CHAPTER 10

2015 – THE UNFORGETTABLE YEAR

At the start of 2015, my twin sister Vera began to have many symptoms, shaking them off like it wasn't anything serious, then the symptoms began to get worse.

The doctors didn't know she had cancer just yet and thought it was an ovarian problem. So they took one ovary out, with the liters of fluid. Then they thought it was stomach cancer. She had some surgery for those two. Then they found a tumor near her colon and that's when they said she had cancer. It's always so sad too because they didn't say much until they could for sure understand what it was. Looking back, at first Vera had shown a few signs of symptoms: Abdominal pain, bloating and blood in her stool. On April 20th, 2015, Vera was diagnosed with colon cancer, stage IV. But I remember as soon I got a phone call that she had cancer and I just balled. Obviously. I couldn't stop crying!

Knowing that my twin sister had cancer was something so saddening and truly alarming. Her official diagnosis was *signet ring cell cancer*. Meaning she had a very rare kind of cancer, especially for her being so young at 25.

I was working at the time and as much as my nanny family said I was free to go to spend time with Vera, she didn't want me to. My nanny family was so supportive but V never wanted me around her worst days. Instead, she kept me updated through phone calls and texting her.

Then right away I started to do what I could for her. Feeling the way I did and feeling for her, it was like a new life for both of us not knowing how long she had.

CHAPTER 11

TEAM VERA

Vera was a strong warrior. Within weeks of her diagnosis, she was being treated in the hospital.

She lived in the hospital for months before she came home. With Vera coming home, I always thought what's next? I tried to do anything possible to care for her as well as make her happy. When she came home, I managed to get our local San Jose Earthquakes soccer team to give her a signed soccer ball. I openly asked friends to write her cards which turned out to be a card shower and ended up having hundreds of cards come to our home, flowers that flooded the room, and even making a sign on our garage door that read Team Vera with a colon cancer awareness ribbon in the middle. Vera's illness suddenly transitioned me into the spotlight.

When Vera was ill, I tried to do whatever I could for her to make her days a bit brighter. Marlene Bjornsrud, who was the general manager of the Bay Area Women's soccer team - The Cyber Rays, and Brandi Chastain went to surprise Vera with a visit a couple of weeks after her diagnosis. They had been a big part of our lives and helped Vera so much. Both Marlene and Brandi are some of the best people we have ever met.

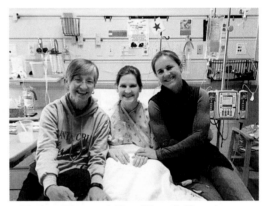

Marlene Bjornsrud, V and Brandi Chastain

Vera, always had a smile on her face and she absolutely took her job at BJ's Brewery more seriously than school, at least that's what we all thought. I remember going through this like it was yesterday. I did what I could for her. Rounds of chemo, she still shined bright and even played 8 games in one week of soccer. Too much? Of course but that was her goal-getter personality. We played many of the games together, other times it was just either her or I and the other one supporting on the sidelines.

In those months we had a powerful twin connection on that soccer field. I would know every soccer move she'd try on me and she never got passed me. It was great when we were on the same team. We were unstoppable! Vera went through a lot and I won't sugar coat it, it was not easy. It's hard on everyone but Vera's personality shined through it all. She made people laugh so hard they cried even on her worst days and she still managed to work at her job, BJ's Brewery. She was an amazing co-worker! She loved every minute of her job! It's what got her through the toughest days ahead.

While we all were sad about Vera's illness, we all tried to make the best of it day by day and just be happy. I remember I had planned to leave on a trip with my boyfriend after going with Vera for her round of chemo early in the morning. At the last minute, my trip was canceled. So instead, my sister, my mom and I left for Disneyland the same day. We walked 8 miles around Disneyland that day. We didn't know then this would be our last Disney trip together.

After that, Vera was in and out of the hospital days and weeks at a time. I remember when Vera didn't want me to be in the hospital room with her while she was being taken care of because she didn't want to see me feeling so sad. I agreed. So I kept on with my coaching job and nanny job at the time.

I was coaching one girl's team at the time and nannying for a wonderful family I had known for some years. This family was so loving, respectful and then and there, I found out, I wanted to work with children later in life. The family I had worked for shared so many memories together. I practically watched the youngest when he started in Kindergarten and as I left my job a few years later, the oldest was starting middle school. They were a one-of-a-kind of a family. I remember the first time we celebrated my birthday with them and the family took me to a very nice dinner out. I felt like this was going to be a wonderful family to work with.

Our last portrait

CHAPTER 12

LOSS: YOU DIE YOUNG

After months of symptoms and chemotherapy, Vera passed away.

At the funeral, the Team Vera sign was displayed and all of her friends signed it. About 500 friends and family attended it. It was a beautiful service. With her favorite animal being a giraffe we even had a friend let us display a 6-foot toy giraffe for her service. People were smiling as they walked in seeing Geoffrey there. She named all her giraffes Geoffrey and we had so many displayed in her room. At the service, we gave out a lot of giraffes to her friends she had kept in her room. With a ballroom full of friends, family and such a bright atmosphere, we even handed out neon green silicone bracelets made with, "There's no offsides in Heaven." (V was always offsides in soccer). I have never seen such a beautiful service. I remember my arms being so tired the next day from hugging hundreds of people that day. I saw many of her friends, peers, classmates, co-workers, teachers who taught her, from all schools and sports coaches! This was for her, and I felt her presence at every moment. We all shared wonderful tributes of our beloved Vera.

'There's no offsides in heaven'

Losing someone so close to you is so hard. It's almost so hard to even explain and every loss is different. Everyone grieves differently too and it simply never gets easier, only a bit better. For me, this loss hit me at all angles. I'd find myself talking to my sister, as she was still with me, I even felt her presence all the time and still today I do. There are things that no one will ever get, only us and that's tough because it's not something you can share with anyone else. The endless memories will forever last in my heart. I think the toughest part about losing someone isn't when death approaches, it's the aftermath. Finding yourself when you've had your other half with you this whole life. For the longest time, I couldn't do things without my sister and I found myself being able to slowly get through it.

Fortunately going through some of the toughest parts of your lives create beautiful things ahead for you. This whole experience being sad, there was some good that came out of it, and as hard as it seems, that's what people have to know. Years after the pain still hurts, and grief never gets easier, but it gets better. You learn to live with it. And everyone grieves in their own way.

While grieving after Vera passed, I actually spoke to her and wanted to have her come "visit" me. I remember after she passed, many friends came up to me and shared many dreams with me. These were not just dreams, they were visits. You can tell when it's a visit because it was so vivid and clear and most visits you will remember them when you wake up. I remember mine perfectly and finally got one from Vera. I remember her looking so beautiful and young as they say, "You die young." I truly believe that.

I think the overall experience is a tough one to handle at any age but when you are so young it is very tough.

Geoffrey was donated to the San Francisco Zoo in Vera's honor.

CHAPTER 13

EXPERIENCING BEING A CAREGIVER

Vera had her whole life ahead of her and that's what struck me hard and continues to affect me. I remember my sister being diagnosed like it was yesterday. Being a twin and having one twin diagnosed at such a young age, you feel a bit guilty that it happened to your other half. We were in shock as a family and I had a roller coaster of emotions to deal with as well as thoughts like – maybe I have colon cancer too. I got tested and was thankful to be okay. Though a colonoscopy is currently recommended for people over 50, I will continue to get checked every five years. Surprisingly colon cancer among the young is on the rise.

Despite being a sad journey, there were many good times we shared. Being twins you have a special bond and you think you can't get any closer but we did get even closer throughout her journey and it brought out the best in me. I was always there to support her even on my worst days. We had an agreement that I would never visit her on bad days in the hospital because she didn't want me to feel bad and I think that's a huge part in why I did so well through her journey because most people would stop their lives to help. And that's fine for some people because people respond to this differently and handle it differently but I know my sister didn't want me to stop going to work, nannying and coaching. Coaching kept me going through this very difficult time. It was a good distraction and one which included my family and friends. We played soccer together when Vera could still play – that helped given the fact that it was an outlet for BOTH of us and played a significantly positive role in our lives.

As a caregiver, I made sure that my sister needed whatever it was at the time, whether she just needed a chat, a simple fast food meal, to play soccer or a car ride to blast her music, I was there. I was her rock, her happy twin when she had some of her worst days, and that's the best part about being a twin. You always have someone there for you. On the other hand, it was tough for me to be there for her and stay positive and composed - because it's tough to witness your loved one's painful journey - but you make the best out of it. That is what some people do realize and do not realize, sometimes it's the caregiver who has the toughest spot in the situation. However, I did feel I had an incredible amount of support and I still feel that way to this day.

Looking back I know going through the loss of my sister was and is tough especially with the outcome we had. Vera was a beautiful person inside and out. Her personality was amazing. She was so strong throughout her journey. I cannot tell you how proud I was of her.

The loss of someone so special hurts you forever but I know she would want me to live for her and be happy.

Our last concert together.
I posted this version after V passed.

CHAPTER 14

2016 – RECOVERY

After Vera's passing passed I took some time off of school after receiving my BA at my Junior College. I remember that I was so excited to graduate and was so proud of all the work I had accomplished which made it all well worth it at the end. I knew then Vera was proud of all the hurdles I overcame and graduated. I traveled the world a bit. Europe, Colorado, and Virginia! Europe was such an amazing trip and I am so glad I was able to explore a new country at such a young age. Many people don't get the privilege to visit other countries. I remember that this trip was beautiful, but at the same time and for the longest time it was hard for me to do something happy when I knew my other half was gone. There were times I felt miserable, because why would I enjoy something when my sister has passed, but then I thought to myself that my sister would only want me to be happy. I took about a year off and then I enrolled in a four-year program to finish my school.

Grief. Yes, grief is something everyone goes through. And everyone grieves differently. You have to let the process take you where it goes, it's like waves in the ocean. Go with it and don't avoid it, but it does get better. My European trip made me realize, in losing my twin sister, there is still so much life ahead of me. With some distance, I could accept all she would want is for me is to be happy, living the best life I can.

Then you also realize other things. Friends. Friends who are there for you and then ones who are not. When someone goes through something like this, you really understand who's there for you. I lost a lot of friends after V passed but have gained so many new friends. "V" is what a lot of us, including me, called her. Vera's passing gave me perspective. I even broke up with a boyfriend at the time but it meant nothing because I just lost my best friend in the world. I learned that every person in my life is so important to me and that you just never realize how close someone is to you until you never see them again. I've come to realize the quantity of friends is less important than the quality. And as you get older, you have fewer friends but it's not a bad thing. It's a process that everyone goes through. Those closest to you will always be there for you. That's just my thoughts.

CHAPTER 15

KEEP MOVING FORWARD

A few months passed and I wanted to continue to do something in honor of my sister. In fact, I felt myself finding things to do has helped me heal in some ways. April following my sister's passing came around, and I spoke at our local Relay for Life. I didn't think I could be a public speaker, but that day I changed many people's lives including mine in a positive way.

Relay for Life is a non-profit organization featuring events such as 24-hour walkathon. The theme is "Cancer doesn't sleep so neither will we." Participants take turns to walk for 24 hours. The organization supports cancer survivors, people who are fighting cancer at the time and family members of those who have passed from this terrible disease. People raise millions of dollars for those in need. It's for a great cause and that people are all trying to find a cure. It was such an amazing experience.

I realize I was meant to share my story with others. I ended up that day speaking at their local event, and that event I was interviewed on our local tv station KTVU. Later that day, when I was done with my speech, I remember hugging my parents so hard and that I started crying because of what I heard. Moments after my speech after the song "Fight Song" by Rachel Platten was playing over the PA. and that just gave me

absolute chills. I hugged some friends and cried. That song brought tears to my eyes. My sister and I heard that song all the time. It's such an uplifting song and an amazing upbeat song to hear when you're going through a rough patch. I remember my sister and I blaring it in our car. It was our song! Just then that buzz came from my phone. I got multiple texts and Facebook posts saying, "I just saw you on TV and little clips sharing your story, it's coming up." I was so shocked! It was happening. I felt like I

was on cloud nine. With the mixed emotions I felt, I was so happy that I truly felt I made a difference that night. It's amazing to think that such a sad ending to a wonderful person, can benefit another and that sharing a powerful story can affect so many. That night I felt my sister's presence and I knew that I would get through this. That TV clip shared my story along with a "Fight Song" video I made which I believe, still viral and still playing. The last time I watched it,
it had over 62,700 views!

CHAPTER 16

2016 – LIFE AFTER LOSS

I raised thousands of dollars for the Relay for Life, The American Cancer Society and even some money for the Colon Cancer Foundation. I was on our local KTVU channel two news for my incredible story which hopefully impacted many. I raised money at a local karaoke bar Vera and I visited nearly every Sunday night. It was an incredible journey along the way however hard at times.

After she had passed I learned to live without someone after living so long with them. She was my best friend in the world. No one got us like we did. I mean learning and reciting lines from every Disney movie that was out there has got to be one of my favorite things about us. No one could relate as we did to each other.

I am learning slowly how to celebrate a birthday after your other half is gone. Do you celebrate? – Do you not? I mean, I remember our 21st and our 25th birthday. Two of the best birthdays shared. Then Vera passed and the first two birthdays were very difficult and I won't lie to you. You feel like you can't celebrate. My third birthday got easier but not the way it was. Perhaps it never will be.

She passed after Christmas and I remember still that Christmas and New Years was a bit sadder that year. Years after, the grief comes and goes and it gets better over time, but never easy. Grief is probably the one thing you simply cannot control, but you need to experience it. While holidays such as our shared Birthday and Christmas come, they also bring back unnecessary and sad memories. You learn to relive their lives through these moments. Each year, the sad memories you do forget about, and then you start to remember more of the happier times. The first Christmas was very hard to experience without her because we had many traditions, but then you learn to make new ones with new friends and family.

While continuing to still coach and playing soccer, I hit a bump in the road in my life. I gained weight. Not that I was obese, but I didn't feel like myself. I have been healthy practically all my life and since my sister passed I made a promise to be healthier. I joined Weight Watchers and lost 30 pounds. This helped me get back on track with my health at least. I joined a personal gym where my trainer provided me with exercises.

I got enough courage to go back doing what I love and that is working out with a personal trainer. About 8 months later I reached my goal and was so proud. Let me give you a little tip, it's great to exercise in fact that's a necessity in my life but the foods you eat are what make your lifestyle overall better for you.

I could not live without soccer or working out and now I eat right too!

CHAPTER 17

LIFE TODAY

Today I continue to coach soccer, two girls team and also coach at John Muir Middle school for the boys and girls program. Coaching kept me going through a lot of this. With such a big passion it was almost as if it was a distraction to keep me going in life. Still today, I play soccer and workout. I also continue to share wonderful stories of my sister Vera to anyone new I meet.

I am currently at San Jose State University finishing up my teaching credential. I plan to make a career of sharing what I have learned – helping each child find their way.

In memory of Vera.

CHAPTER 18

FINDING FAITH AND HOPE

I'm sure you are wondering why I named the book, "Finding Faith and Hope". When we were little we *found* each other at the orphanage, grew up as best friends, and lived wonderful lives together. We had one another through those rough times. While coming to grips with grief after the death of my twin, I am finding myself along the way.

I had my twin with me all the way until adulthood. Now that she is gone, I am learning to find Faith and in myself, Hope. It's like I gave her Faith, and now she's giving me Hope. Life isn't meant to be always a happy journey, but if you're hopeful it can get better. It can. It's so important to make every day, moment and memory count. You will be one step in the right direction so that any kind of obstacle life throws you, know you can find a way through it. I'll tell you what I tell myself through hard times, keep moving forward – always.

"Finding Faith and Hope" also comes from our Russian names. The Russian word for *faith* is vera and nadya means *hope*. In Russian culture daughters are often named in a trilogy; Hope, Faith and the third person is called Love. But we were only twins so it was set as Faith and Hope. For the longest time, I never told anyone about my real name. I didn't think much of it at the time.

Sunflowers were our favorite. I took the cover photos in one of the many fields in California. Anytime I see one, I can feel Vera with me.

I remain hopeful that I will be able to honor Vera with a long, wonderful life. We had such a unique background growing up that made us who we are today.

UNSTOPPABLE

CHAPTER 19

AFTERTHOUGHTS

Adoption

If you are thinking about adoption, I hope I've inspired you to do so, it was a beautiful journey our parents experienced, as well as us and today, even though Vera is gone, we are forever grateful for the parents who gave us hope, strength, , and courage. There were ups and downs in learning ways to get through things, but all have been worth it. Adoption is a beautiful thing for anyone to do, and there are hundreds and hundreds of children that are in need of a home. I still wonder what growing up with Russian parents would have been like since I never met my birth parents, but I know I love my adoptive parents just as much. It doesn't matter at all if you're adopted, you are still considered to be a family. Someone who takes you in, cares for you, believes in you, respects and loves you, is family. I met mine, the day my twin sister and I were adopted.

Being a Twin:

There is so much to experience as a twin whether it be silly things such as fighting, or having a close empathetic bond you share. Twins fight just like any other siblings and some time over the dumbest things and I mean dumb! I remember Vera would always steal my clothes to wear. I didn't care that much if she took them but she'd do it in a way where she'd be sneaky about it. That was the part I was mad about. She never asked! I remember having locks put on our doors, but that never worked. I also remember fighting over who would be first in line or who would go first. These things would drive my parents crazy!

We also had an intimate bond where when one knew we were upset, the other would feel upset too. It is a real thing like *twin empathy*. We also had our own twin dialogue and it's true. We'd always end up saying the same thing at the exact same time.

Learning to Move Forward:

You know, even being a twin you still need to be able to be yourself. I think when she passed my hardest challenges are these: First I had to adjust to is doing things by myself. Having always had someone. Always. That sensation never goes away and always will be tough. The second? Learning to live life without her. Vera was always there to help me learn new things. If it hadn't been for her, I'd never have pushed myself to be so outgoing. She was the icebreaker to conversations and helped me feel comfortable in coming out of my shell. My personality has become stronger. Life is so precious and you never know when it will be taken away. So live! I live for her ever day and continue to shine every day for her. She may be gone, but she will always live in my heart.

Last words – for Now:

Something Vera said to keep her spirits high every day, especially through her cancer. "There are no bad days in life, only bad moments." I have learned to see the beauty in each day.

The story I have shared here hopefully gave you a sense of how my sister and I lived life for each other. Despite the obstacles we both faced, they made us stronger. Powerful and unique moments that were shared and experienced in Russia, sculptured us to be who we were meant to be – Strong and Beautiful.

With Faith and Hope,

Nadya

Nadya.

Made in the USA
Middletown, DE
02 January 2020